Praise for Joseph Lease

"Joseph Lease's is a singularly moving and devastatingly beautiful voice in contemporary poetry. The haunting iterations and luminous specificity of his powerful new collection, *The Body Ghost,* channel the sadness, rage, and desire of this fraught historical moment in a vibrant minor key. Lease's musical repetition is a site of political awakening; a site of hope, demolition, and mourning: 'we made / this sky of drones to eat your voice,' 'lavender sky, sky like whiskey—the way, the way / we live in bodies.' Flipping between one version of reality and its repetition evokes a gap of inequality within the lyric self which cleaves and doubles its singing: 'you didn't, you did.' Lease's stunning poetry is simultaneously a solid, a liquid, and a gas, its acrobatics and multivocal simultaneity offering models for examining everything from privilege and property to the poignant death of a family member. And at its center, always, is a beating heart."

—Trace Peterson

"I really don't know how Joseph Lease does this. Reaches such lyric heights with such delicacy. With skillful use of anaphora, and perfect, various, open-verse forms transformed page to page, Lease is a tour de force master of prosody, of the subtle music of words evoking, in this case, passionate feelings of caring, of grief, of sorrow for this broken world. These poems are unique; nothing I have read is like them."

—Norman Fischer

"*The Body Ghost* is part of a body of work that is significant and reveals Joseph Lease to be a major force in contemporary American literature."

—Sheila Murphy

"These poems, rife with music and sly, playful inquiries into the world, have some of Frank O'Hara's metropolitan freshness and directness; they're charming in their artful, lyrical gestures ('the elegies / are taking off their clothes'), but also plangent at key moments in their genuine moral and social critique ('tear up maps— / democracy is anybody's eyes—feel / like you might have, might have / killed someone'). Yes, *The Body Ghost* is a spectral fan dance or a poetic striptease of sorts— its haunted, incremental engines, lavish white spaces, and agile floating lines (like tracks in amassed snow sometimes), its neo-Dickinson dashes leading the entranced reader toward revelatory clues, needling truths, and insistent joys."

—Cyrus Cassells

The Body
Ghost

Also by Joseph Lease

Broken World

Testify

The Body Ghost

POEMS BY JOSEPH LEASE

COFFEE HOUSE PRESS
Minneapolis
2018

Coffee House Press books are available to the trade through
our primary distributor, Consortium Book Sales & Distribution,
cbsd.com or (800) 283-3572. For personal orders, catalogs, or
other information, write to info@coffeehousepress.org.

Coffee House Press is a nonprofit literary publishing house.
Support from private foundations, corporate giving programs,
government programs, and generous individuals helps make the
publication of our books possible. We gratefully acknowledge
their support in detail in the back of this book.

LIBRARY OF CONGRESS CATALOGING-IN-PUBLICATION DATA

Names: Lease, Joseph, author.
Title: The body ghost : poems / Joseph Lease.
Description: Minneapolis : Coffee House Press, 2018.
Identifiers: LCCN 2017040749 | ISBN 9781566895118 (trade pbk.)
Classification: LCC PS3562.E255 A6 2018 | DDC 811/.54—dc23
LC record available at https://lccn.loc.gov/2017040749

Printed in the United States of America

25 24 23 22 21 20 19 18   2 3 4 5 6 7 8 9

For Chris Fischbach

The Body
Ghost

Ritual

1

the light that's burning every second now—

say *moon,* say *ink,* say *stay in love*—and eyes

are masks and masks are eyes—say *moon,*

say *ink,* say *stay in love*—

2

once more I smell the dew and rain—the

light that's burning everything—the elegies

are taking off their clothes—say *moon*, say

ink, say *stay in love*—

3

and some guy screams on Christmas Eve—

his eyes like rain, his face like ice—and

weave a circle round him thrice—we drink

to death, we smear the sky—soft wind—the

soul beneath the soul beneath the soul—

4

he fell apart, he rained, he flew, he sang—

and some guy screams on Christmas Eve—

we drink to death, we smear the dark—blue

wind—his stain of faded storm light in my

mouth—

Mercy

1

pink streaks,

sky, pink streaks, branches—buildings

turn purple—the wind sings the moon—

the moon sings the wind—all the words,

all the worlds, in one face—

2

one story—the boy and the wren—the

wren and the night—the face in the

house—your lips slip the night—your

face slips your eyes—your eyes slip

your *yes*—love like flying—

3

where is your kiss—who is your night—

smile painting, smile sacred arcs of

rain—O taste, O taste and see—I can't

believe we've come to this—you rose—I

can't believe—

4

and all the words—all the hands—you

dream me—dream me there—soft mist,

soft kiss—mend the world—maybe it's

possible—what do you know—what do

you taste: vodka, ice, soft air, soft air—

your hands—what if I worship you—

your life is real—

5

tonight—what's that—your voice, your

wing—tonight can sing tomorrow's

ring—arc, arc me the secret—your

gaze, soft moon—you go so deep—your

sound, your sound—you go so deep—

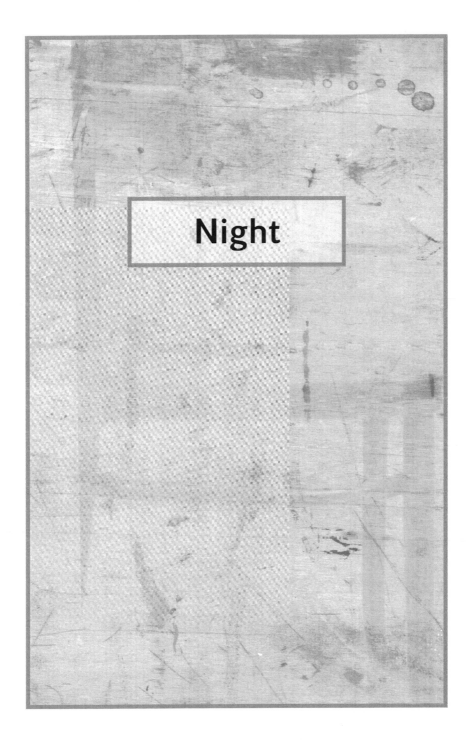

Night

Night

does he

like bombs, does he like masks—please

breathe my newsflash, my eyes don't fit—

sound gives life—death's sound too—

before you broke me I thought I was free:

sinful but free—

Night

breathe me morn and mourn me when:

everything said the house: death said

the house, the house said death, death

said everything:

Night

I tore the page—I tore up the page—I had to,

I had to—makc words   the truth slipped—I

touched it—vodka to hoping, hoping to open,

roses and glisten—listen and listen—

Night

so run around like daydreams, tear

up maps—democracy is anybody's

eyes—to lie, to lie, to lie, to lie—

please breathe my newsflash, my

eyes don't fit—

Night

I was kissing what you wrote: and you

were lost and found, and you were

trains and rings: lights, camera,

courage:

Night

just breathe night, breathe night forever—just

say drop your eyes right here—"quick, learn to

die"—I'm dancing—I'm praying—I'm breathing—

I'm nothing—I'm snow—I'm falling—pigeons

fight for chicken wings—

Night

lights, camera, courage: I was kissing

what you wrote—each peaches, each

amazing, each: so always, so yes, so

never say never, so always, so yes, I

want to believe:

The Body Ghost

I tore

the page,

I tore

up the

page

you give me love because you give

me love: you give me up because

you give me up: the light is real

because the real is light: the real

is light because the light is real:

any purple day: the world is gone,

the world is back:

and to

your

scattered

bodies go

bless anyone

bless anyone

all

night

I was

your hair

The Body Ghost

property is death: they had a body crammed in

a mailbox and it was just a blue suit with bones

sticking out—and fathers lost in blowing snow—

and mothers drift in blowing leaves—and all the

lies in any town—work was my salvation, he said,

work was always my salvation

branches

you

joy can

scream

ice and the river—"the desire to be normal is healthy":

no, it isn't—can you imagine the death of the wind—

can you remember the ghost of that voice—

your

    kisses

your

    sky

your

    darkness

your

    sky

lavender sky, sky like whiskey—the way, the way

we live in bodies—lavender sky, sky like whiskey—

and to your scattered bodies go—your dream inside

your face, your night inside your morning—I'll try

to glint like birds behind the rain—

Rent Is Theft

Rent Is Theft

this sky is your sky this

sky is my sky—"Dear God

let there be gas let there

be cash and soft voices"

Rent Is Theft

hide me

among

the graves: the city, the wind, the banks:

"you just want to die I mean capitalism

just wants to kill you I mean you just

want and you just want"—

Rent Is Theft

"we made

this sky of drones to eat your voice"—

"the sky is money, privatize the sky"—

your ocean dies, and Google buys the

sun inside your name—

Rent Is Theft

they had a body crammed in a mailbox

and it was just a blue suit with

bones sticking out—

Rent Is Theft

you didn't, you did: just keep shopping—

eyes was I, dawn breaking, earth breathing:

just say missiles, just say drones: frack,

baby, frack: my eyes are made of cash and

going broke

Rent Is Theft

we never drove the blue car through

the stars:

we always drove the blue car through

the stars:

we never guessed the dream we never

guessed:

we always guessed the dream we

always guessed:

today we fight like gods, today we fight

for gods,

how much is that ahi in the window,

here you are, here we are, no mercy,

no future, lots and lots of turkey

sausage,

death tangles, death shakes, death

breakfast served all night,

death tangles, death shakes,

death-flavored ice cream, deathberry

gum—

Rent Is Theft

so run around

like daydreams, tear up maps—

democracy is anybody's eyes—feel

like you might have, might have,

killed someone:

Rent Is Theft

you didn't, you did: just keep shopping—

and promise me the rich can't sleep—

and promise me the rich can't sleep—

Rent Is Theft

please please please be ironic—we left

our freedom in "American" mouths, we

broke our freedom in "American" words—

you run around like daydreams, tear up

maps, democracy is anybody's eyes—

Rent Is Theft

we left

our freedom in "American" mouths,

we broke our freedom in "American"

words—tell me—will I spark—in this

light, expensive light—did you pray—

did you beg—for days

like these—

Rent Is Theft

wake up, you're not the truth—and,

and, and, and—I, I, I, I—might have,

killed someone: you didn't, you did:

eyes was I,

Rent Is Theft

just keep shopping—I could've

been one hundred years of war,

I could've been one hundred

years of peace: frack, baby,

frack: my eyes are made of cash

and going broke

Lights Out

and what

you

want is

what

you want

(not

really), and

what

you

want

is

what you

want

(till Tuesday),

and

where you

go

is where

you

went

(forget it),

and coffee

tastes like

evidence

(don't let it):

and holy

    is as

        holy does,

and holy

    tastes

        like ruby

walls, and

    rivers

paint

you wind

and

snow,

and

houses

you will

never know—

Stay

"when I

squeeze

your

hand I'm

squeezing her

hand"

his mother

in the

room—

his mother's

me—

He's dying—

    He's dying—

He's asking

    Why

I

    Love

Him—

"when I

squeeze

your

hand I'm

squeezing her

hand"

the

    whiskey on

the table, the

    rabbits in the

yard at

    night—

my father

rain

becoming

rain

rain

becoming

rain

"even

when I

don't see

you, I'll

see you"

He's dying—

    He's dying—

He's asking

    Why

I

    Love

Him—

his

stain of

faded

storm

light in

my mouth:

The Body Ghost

someone

scatters

someone's

body:

ashes,

ashes,

let's fall

down,

      just some

      hours and

just some

clown,

now

      you

eat your

spiderweb,

now you

dance

inside

your bed,

go and

go and

go ahead:

"and

may

the wind

that killed

you

slide

you

home"—

Acknowledgments

These poems were written between 2010 and 2015.

Grateful acknowledgment is made to the editors of the journals and anthologies in which these poems first appeared: the *Brooklyn Rail, Colorado Review, Denver Quarterly, Litscapes: Collected US Writings 2015, New American Writing, Nouveau's Midnight Sun,* and *OmniVerse.* The Academy of American Poets anthologized "The Body Ghost (property is death)" on *poets.org* and made it a part of its Poem-a-Day series. One poem in this book uses one short phrase from Herbert and one short phrase from Coleridge; two poems in this book use one short phrase from Donne. The author wishes to thank California College of the Arts for making the writing of this book possible through the generous awarding of a faculty research sabbatical grant.

"Mercy" is for Donna de la Perrière.

Coffee House Press began as a small letterpress operation in 1972 and has grown into an internationally renowned nonprofit publisher of literary fiction, essay, poetry, and other work that doesn't fit neatly into genre categories.

Coffee House is both a publisher and an arts organization. Through our *Books in Action* program and publications, we've become interdisciplinary collaborators and incubators for new work and audience experiences. Our vision for the future is one where a publisher is a catalyst and connector.

LITERATURE
is not the same thing as
PUBLISHING

FUNDER ACKNOWLEDGMENTS

Coffee House Press is an internationally renowned independent book publisher and arts nonprofit based in Minneapolis, MN; through its literary publications and *Books in Action* program, Coffee House acts as a catalyst and connector— between authors and readers, ideas and resources, creativity and community, inspiration and action.

Coffee House Press books are made possible through the generous support of grants and donations from corporations, state and federal grant programs, family foundations, and the many individuals who believe in the transformational power of literature. This activity is made possible by the voters of Minnesota through a Minnesota State Arts Board Operating Support grant, thanks to the legislative appropriation from the arts and cultural heritage fund. Coffee House also receives major operating support from the Amazon Literary Partnership, the Jerome Foundation, The McKnight Foundation, Target Foundation, and the National Endowment for the Arts (NEA). To find out more about how NEA grants impact individuals and communities, visit www.arts.gov.

Coffee House Press receives additional support from the Elmer L. & Eleanor J. Andersen Foundation; the David & Mary Anderson Family Foundation; the Buuck Family Foundation; Fredrikson & Byron, P.A.; Dorsey & Whitney LLP; the Fringe Foundation; Kenneth Koch Literary Estate; the Knight Foundation; the Rehael Fund of the Minneapolis Foundation; the Matching Grant Program Fund of the Minneapolis Foundation; Mr. Pancks' Fund in memory of Graham Kimpton; the Schwab Charitable Fund; Schwegman, Lundberg & Woessner, P.A.; the U.S. Bank Foundation; VSA Minnesota for the Metropolitan Regional Arts Council; and the Woessner Freeman Family Foundation in honor of Allan Kornblum.

THE PUBLISHER'S CIRCLE OF COFFEE HOUSE PRESS

Publisher's Circle members make significant contributions to Coffee House Press's annual giving campaign. Understanding that a strong financial base is necessary for the press to meet the challenges and opportunities that arise each year, this group plays a crucial part in the success of Coffee House's mission.

Recent Publisher's Circle members include many anonymous donors, Suzanne Allen, Patricia A. Beithon, the E. Thomas Binger & Rebecca Rand Fund of the Minneapolis Foundation, Robert & Gail Buuck, Claire Casey, Louise Copeland, Jane Dalrymple-Hollo, Mary Ebert & Paul Stembler, Kaywin Feldman & Jim Lutz, Chris Fischbach & Katie Dublinski, Sally French, Jocelyn Hale & Glenn Miller, the Rehael Fund-Roger Hale/Nor Hall of the Minneapolis Foundation, Randy Hartten & Ron Lotz, Dylan Hicks & Nina Hale, William Hardacker, Jeffrey Hom, Carl & Heidi Horsch, Amy L. Hubbard & Geoffrey J. Kehoe Fund, Kenneth Kahn & Susan Dicker, Stephen & Isabel Keating, Kenneth Koch Literary Estate, Cinda Kornblum, Jennifer Kwon Dobbs & Stefan Liess, Lenfestey Family Foundation, Sarah Lutman & Rob Rudolph, the Carol & Aaron Mack Charitable Fund of the Minneapolis Foundation, George & Olga Mack, Joshua Mack & Ron Warren, Gillian McCain, Mary & Malcolm McDermid, Sjur Midness & Briar Andresen, Maureen Millea Smith & Daniel Smith, Peter Nelson & Jennifer Swenson, Enrique & Jennifer Olivarez, Alan Polsky, Marc Porter & James Hennessy, Robin Preble, Alexis Scott, Ruth Stricker Dayton, Jeffrey Sugerman & Sarah Schultz, Nan G. & Stephen C. Swid, Patricia Tilton, Joanne Von Blon, Stu Wilson & Melissa Barker, Warren D. Woessner & Iris C. Freeman, Margaret Wurtele, and Wayne P. Zink & Christopher Schout.

For more information about the Publisher's Circle
and other ways to support Coffee House Press books, authors,
and activities, please visit www.coffeehousepress.org/support
or contact us at info@coffeehousepress.org.

Joseph Lease's critically acclaimed books of poetry include *Testify* (Coffee House Press, 2011) and *Broken World* (Coffee House Press, 2007). His poems have appeared in many anthologies, including *Postmodern American Poetry: A Norton Anthology* and *The Best American Poetry*. He is a professor of writing and literature at California College of the Arts and lives in Oakland with the poet Donna de la Perrière.

The Body Ghost was designed by
Bookmobile Design & Digital Publisher Services.
Text is set in Bookman Old Style Pro.